THIS JOURNAL BELONGS TO:

_____

JOURNAL THROUGH THE

NEW TESTAMENT

- IN ONE YEAR -

DAY 1

Matthew 1

DAY 2

Matthew 2

DAY 3

Matthew 3

DAY 4

Matthew 4

DAY 5

Matthew 5:1-20

_____

_____

_____

_____

_____

_____

_____

_____

_____

_____

_____

_____

_____

_____

_____

_____

_____

_____

_____

_____

_____

_____

DAY 6

Matthew 5:21-48

DAY 7

Matthew 6:1-18

DAY 8

Matthew 6:19-34

DAY 9

Matthew 7

DAY 10

Matthew 8:1-17

_____
_____
_____
_____
_____
_____
_____
_____
_____
_____
_____
_____
_____
_____
_____
_____
_____
_____
_____
_____
_____
_____
_____

DAY 11

Matthew 8:18-34

DAY 12

Matthew 9:1-17

DAY 13

Matthew 9:18-38

DAY 14

Matthew 10:1-15

DAY 15

Matthew 10:16-42

DAY 16

Matthew 11

DAY 17

Matthew 12:1-21

_____

_____

_____

_____

_____

_____

_____

_____

_____

_____

_____

_____

_____

_____

_____

_____

_____

_____

_____

_____

_____

_____

_____

_____

DAY 18

Matthew 12:22-50

DAY 19

Matthew 13:1-33

DAY 20

Matthew 13:34-58

DAY 21

Matthew 14:1-21

DAY 22

Matthew 14:22-36

DAY 23

Matthew 15:1-20

_____
_____
_____
_____
_____
_____
_____
_____
_____
_____
_____
_____
_____
_____
_____
_____
_____
_____
_____
_____
_____

DAY 24

Matthew 15:21-39

DAY 25

Matthew 16

DAY 26

Matthew 17

DAY 27

Matthew 18:1-20

DAY 28

Matthew 18:21-35

DAY 29

Matthew 19

DAY 30

Matthew 20:1-19

_____
_____
_____
_____
_____
_____
_____
_____
_____
_____
_____
_____
_____
_____
_____
_____
_____
_____
_____
_____
_____
_____
_____
_____
_____
_____
_____

DAY 31

Matthew 20:20-34

DAY 32

Matthew 21:1-22

DAY 33

Matthew 21:23-46

DAY 34

Matthew 22:1-22

_____
_____
_____
_____
_____
_____
_____
_____
_____
_____
_____
_____
_____
_____
_____
_____
_____
_____
_____
_____
_____
_____
_____

DAY 35

Matthew 22:23-46

DAY 36

Matthew 23:1-22

_____

_____

_____

_____

_____

_____

_____

_____

_____

_____

_____

_____

_____

_____

_____

_____

_____

_____

_____

_____

_____

DAY 37

Matthew 23:23-39

DAY 38

Matthew 24:1-28

DAY 39

Matthew 24:29-51

DAY 40

Matthew 25:1-30

_____

_____

_____

_____

_____

_____

_____

_____

_____

_____

_____

_____

_____

_____

_____

_____

_____

_____

_____

_____

DAY 41

Matthew 25:31-46

DAY 42

Matthew 26:1-35

DAY 43

Matthew 26:36-75

_____

_____

_____

_____

_____

_____

_____

_____

_____

_____

_____

_____

_____

_____

_____

_____

_____

_____

_____

_____

_____

DAY 44

Matthew 27:1-31

DAY 45

Matthew 27:32-66

DAY 46

Matthew 28

DAY 47

Mark 1:1-20

DAY 48

Mark 1:21-45

_____
_____
_____
_____
_____
_____
_____
_____
_____
_____
_____
_____
_____
_____
_____
_____
_____
_____
_____
_____
_____
_____
_____
_____
_____
_____
_____
_____

DAY 49

Mark 2

DAY 50

Mark 3:1-21

_____
_____
_____
_____
_____
_____
_____
_____
_____
_____
_____
_____
_____
_____
_____
_____
_____
_____
_____
_____
_____
_____
_____
_____
_____

DAY 51

Mark 3:22-35

DAY 52

Mark 4:1-20

DAY 53

Mark 4:21-41

DAY 54

Mark 5:1-20

DAY 55

Mark 5:21-43

DAY 56

Mark 6:1-29

DAY 57

Mark 6:30-56

DAY 58

Mark 7:1-23

DAY 59

Mark 7:24-37

DAY 60

Mark 8:1-21

DAY 61

Mark 8:22-9:1

DAY 62

Mark 9:2-29

DAY 63

Mark 9:30-50

DAY 64

Mark 10:1-31

DAY 65

Mark 10:32-52

DAY 66

Mark 11:1-14

DAY 67

Mark 11:15-33

DAY 68

Mark 12:1-27

_____
_____
_____
_____
_____
_____
_____
_____
_____
_____
_____
_____
_____
_____
_____
_____
_____
_____
_____
_____
_____
_____
_____
_____

DAY 69

Mark 12:28-44

DAY 70

Mark 13:1-23

_____

_____

_____

_____

_____

_____

_____

_____

_____

_____

_____

_____

_____

_____

_____

_____

_____

_____

_____

_____

_____

_____

_____

DAY 71
Mark 13:24-37

DAY 72

Mark 14:1-31

_____

_____

_____

_____

_____

_____

_____

_____

_____

_____

_____

_____

_____

_____

_____

_____

_____

_____

_____

_____

_____

_____

_____

_____

_____

DAY 73

Mark 14:32-72

DAY 74

Mark 15:1-20

DAY 75

Mark 15:21-47

DAY 76

Mark 16

DAY 77

Luke 1:1-38

_____
_____
_____
_____
_____
_____
_____
_____
_____
_____
_____
_____
_____
_____
_____
_____
_____
_____
_____
_____
_____
_____
_____
_____
_____

DAY 78

Luke 1:39-80

DAY 79

Luke 2:1-21

DAY 80

Luke 2:22-52

_____
_____
_____
_____
_____
_____
_____
_____
_____
_____
_____
_____
_____
_____
_____
_____
_____
_____
_____
_____
_____
_____
_____
_____

DAY 81

Luke 3:1-22

DAY 82

Luke 3:23-38

DAY 83

Luke 4:1-30

DAY 84

Luke 4:31-44

DAY 85

Luke 5:1-16

DAY 86

Luke 5:17-39

_____

_____

_____

_____

_____

_____

_____

_____

_____

_____

_____

_____

_____

_____

_____

_____

_____

_____

_____

_____

_____

_____

_____

_____

DAY 87

Luke 6:1-26

DAY 88

Luke 6:27-49

DAY 89

Luke 7:1-35

DAY 90

Luke 7:36-50

_____
_____
_____
_____
_____
_____
_____
_____
_____
_____
_____
_____
_____
_____
_____
_____
_____
_____
_____
_____
_____
_____
_____

DAY 91

Luke 8:1-25

DAY 92

Luke 8:26-56

_____
_____
_____
_____
_____
_____
_____
_____
_____
_____
_____
_____
_____
_____
_____
_____
_____
_____
_____
_____
_____
_____
_____
_____
_____
_____
_____

DAY 93

Luke 9:1-27

_____

_____

_____

_____

_____

_____

_____

_____

_____

_____

_____

_____

_____

_____

_____

_____

_____

_____

_____

_____

_____

_____

_____

DAY 94

Luke 9:28-62

DAY 95

Luke 10:1-20

DAY 96

Luke 10:21-42

_____
_____
_____
_____
_____
_____
_____
_____
_____
_____
_____
_____
_____
_____
_____
_____
_____
_____
_____
_____
_____
_____
_____
_____
_____
_____
_____
_____

DAY 97

Luke 11:1-26

DAY 98

Luke 11:27-54

DAY 99

Luke 12:1-34

DAY 100

Luke 12:35-59

DAY 101

Luke 13:1-17

DAY 102

Luke 13:18-35

DAY 103

Luke 14:1-24

DAY 104

Luke 14:25-35

DAY 105

Luke 15:1-10

DAY 106

Luke 15:11-32

_____
_____
_____
_____
_____
_____
_____
_____
_____
_____
_____
_____
_____
_____
_____
_____
_____
_____
_____
_____
_____
_____
_____
_____
_____
_____

DAY 107

Luke 16:1-17

DAY 108

Luke 16:18-31

DAY 109

Luke 17:1-19

DAY 110

Luke 17:20-37

DAY 111

Luke 18:1-17

DAY 112

Luke 18:18-43

DAY 113

Luke 19:1-27

_____
_____
_____
_____
_____
_____
_____
_____
_____
_____
_____
_____
_____
_____
_____
_____
_____
_____
_____
_____
_____

DAY 114

Luke 19:28-48

_____
_____
_____
_____
_____
_____
_____
_____
_____
_____
_____
_____
_____
_____
_____
_____
_____
_____
_____
_____
_____
_____
_____
_____
_____
_____

DAY 115

Luke 20:1-26

DAY 116

Luke 20:27-47

DAY 117

Luke 21:1-19

DAY 118

Luke 21:20-38

DAY 119

Luke 22:1-34

DAY 120

Luke 22:35-71

DAY 121

Luke 23:1-25

DAY 122

Luke 23:26-56

DAY 123

Luke 24:1-35

DAY 124

Luke 24:36-53

DAY 125

John 1:1-28

DAY 126

John 1:29-51

DAY 127

John 2

DAY 128

John 3:1-15

DAY 129

John 3:16-36

DAY 130

John 4:1-26

DAY 131

John 4:27-54

DAY 132

John 5:1-29

_____
_____
_____
_____
_____
_____
_____
_____
_____
_____
_____
_____
_____
_____
_____
_____
_____
_____
_____
_____
_____
_____
_____

DAY 133

John 5:30-47

DAY 134

John 6:1-21

_____
_____
_____
_____
_____
_____
_____
_____
_____
_____
_____
_____
_____
_____
_____
_____
_____
_____
_____
_____
_____
_____
_____
_____
_____

DAY 135

John 6:22-59

DAY 136

John 6:60-7:24

DAY 137

John 7:25-52

DAY 138

John 7:53-8:30

_____
_____
_____
_____
_____
_____
_____
_____
_____
_____
_____
_____
_____
_____
_____
_____
_____
_____
_____
_____
_____
_____
_____
_____
_____
_____

DAY 139

John 8:31-59

DAY 140

John 9:1-17

DAY 141

John 9:18-41

DAY 142

John 10:1-21

DAY 143

John 10:22-42

DAY 144

John 11:1-27

DAY 145

John 11:28-57

DAY 146

John 12:1-26

DAY 147

John 12:27-50

DAY 148

John 13:1-20

_____
_____
_____
_____
_____
_____
_____
_____
_____
_____
_____
_____
_____
_____
_____
_____
_____
_____
_____
_____
_____
_____
_____
_____
_____

DAY 149

John 13:21-38

DAY 150

John 14:1-14

_____

_____

_____

_____

_____

_____

_____

_____

_____

_____

_____

_____

_____

_____

_____

_____

_____

_____

_____

_____

_____

_____

_____

DAY 151

John 14:15-31

DAY 152

John 15:1-17

DAY 153

John 15:18–16:15

DAY 154

John 16:16-33

DAY 155

John 17

DAY 156

John 18:1-27

DAY 157

John 18:28-40

DAY 158

John 19:1-27

DAY 159

John 19:28-42

DAY 160

John 20:1-18

DAY 161

John 20:19-31

DAY 162

John 21

DAY 163

Acts 1

DAY 164

Acts 2:1-13

DAY 165

Acts 2:14-47

DAY 166

Acts 3

DAY 167

Acts 4:1-22

DAY 168

Acts 4:23-37

DAY 169

Acts 5:1-16

DAY 170

Acts 5:17-42

DAY 171

Acts 6

DAY 172

Acts 7:1-29

DAY 173

Acts 7:30-60

DAY 174

Acts 8:1-25

DAY 175

Acts 8:26-40

DAY 176

Acts 9:1-22

_____
_____
_____
_____
_____
_____
_____
_____
_____
_____
_____
_____
_____
_____
_____
_____
_____
_____
_____
_____
_____
_____
_____
_____
_____
_____

DAY 177

Acts 9:23-43

DAY 178

Acts 10:1-33

DAY 179

Acts 10:34-48

DAY 180

Acts 11

DAY 181

Acts 12

DAY 182

Acts 13:1-12

_____
_____
_____
_____
_____
_____
_____
_____
_____
_____
_____
_____
_____
_____
_____
_____
_____
_____
_____
_____
_____
_____
_____
_____
_____
_____
_____
_____

DAY 183

Acts 13:13-52

DAY 184

Acts 14

_____

_____

_____

_____

_____

_____

_____

_____

_____

_____

_____

_____

_____

_____

_____

_____

_____

_____

_____

_____

_____

_____

_____

_____

_____

DAY 185

Acts 15:1-21

DAY 186

Acts 15:22-41

DAY 187

Acts 16:1-15

DAY 188

acts 16:16-40

DAY 189

Acts 17:1-15

DAY 190

Acts 17:16-34

DAY 191

Acts 18

DAY 192

Acts 19:1-20

_____
_____
_____
_____
_____
_____
_____
_____
_____
_____
_____
_____
_____
_____
_____
_____
_____
_____
_____
_____
_____
_____
_____
_____
_____
_____
_____

DAY 193

Acts 19::21-41

DAY 194

Acts 20:1-16

_____

_____

_____

_____

_____

_____

_____

_____

_____

_____

_____

_____

_____

_____

_____

_____

_____

_____

_____

_____

_____

_____

_____

DAY 195

Acts 20:17-38

DAY 196

Acts 21:1-26

DAY 197

Acts 21:27-36

DAY 198

Acts 21:37–22:29

_____
_____
_____
_____
_____
_____
_____
_____
_____
_____
_____
_____
_____
_____
_____
_____
_____
_____
_____
_____
_____
_____
_____
_____
_____

DAY 199

Acts 22:30-23:11

DAY 200

Acts 23:12-35

DAY 201

Acts 24

DAY 202

Acts 25:

DAY 203

Acts 26:1-11

_____

_____

_____

_____

_____

_____

_____

_____

_____

_____

_____

_____

_____

_____

_____

_____

_____

_____

_____

_____

_____

_____

DAY 204

Acts 26:12-32

DAY 205

Acts 27:1-12

DAY 206

Acts 27:13-44

DAY 207

Acts 28:1-16

DAY 208

Acts 28:17-31

DAY 209

Romans 1:1-17

DAY 210

romans 1:18-32

DAY 211

Romans 2

DAY 212

Romans 3:1-20

DAY 213

Romans 3:21-31

DAY 214

Romans 4

_____

_____

_____

_____

_____

_____

_____

_____

_____

_____

_____

_____

_____

_____

_____

_____

_____

_____

_____

_____

_____

_____

_____

_____

_____

DAY 215

Romans 5

DAY 216

Romans 6

DAY 217

Romans 7

DAY 218

Romans 8:1-17

DAY 219

Romans 8:18-39

DAY 220
Romans 9

DAY 221

Romans 10

DAY 222

Romans 11

DAY 223

Romans 12

DAY 224

Romans 13

DAY 225

Romans 14

DAY 226

Romans 15

_____
_____
_____
_____
_____
_____
_____
_____
_____
_____
_____
_____
_____
_____
_____
_____
_____
_____
_____
_____
_____
_____
_____

DAY 227

Romans 16

DAY 228

1 Corinthians 1:1-17

DAY 229

1 Corinthians 1:18-31

DAY 230

1 Corinthians 2

DAY 231

1 Corinthians 3

DAY 232

1 Corinthians 4

DAY 233

1 Corinthians 5

DAY 234

1 Corinthians 6

DAY 235

1 Corinthians 7:1-16

DAY 236

1 Corinthians 7:17-40

DAY 237

1 Corinthians 8

DAY 238

1 Corinthians 9

DAY 239

1 Corinthians 10:1-22

DAY 240

1 Corinthians 10:23-11:1

DAY 241

1 Corinthians 11:2-16

DAY 242

1 Corinthians 11:17-34

DAY 243

1 Corinthians 12:1-11

DAY 244

1 Corinthians 12:12-31

DAY 245

1 Corinthians 13

DAY 246

1 Corinthians 14:1-25

DAY 247

1 Corinthians 14:26-40

DAY 248

1 Corinthians 15:1-34

DAY 249

1 Corinthians 15:35-58

DAY 250

1 Corinthians 16

DAY 251

2 Corinthians 1

DAY 252

2 Corinthians 2

DAY 253

2 Corinthians 3

DAY 254

2 Corinthians 4

_____

_____

_____

_____

_____

_____

_____

_____

_____

_____

_____

_____

_____

_____

_____

_____

_____

_____

_____

_____

_____

DAY 255

2 Corinthians 51:1-10

DAY 256

2 Corinthians 5:11–6:13

DAY 257

2 Corinthians 6:14–7:16

DAY 258

2 Corinthians 8

DAY 259

2 Corinthians 9

DAY 260

2 Corinthians 10

DAY 261

2 Corinthians 11

DAY 262

2 Corinthians 12

DAY 263

2 Corinthians 13

DAY 264

Galatians 1

DAY 265

Galatians 2

DAY 266

Galatians 3

DAY 267

Galatians 4

DAY 268

Galatians 5

DAY 269

Galatians 6

DAY 270

Ephesians 1

DAY 271

Ephesians 2

DAY 272

Ephesians 3

DAY 273

Ephesians 4:1-16

DAY 274

Ephesians 4:17-32

_____
_____
_____
_____
_____
_____
_____
_____
_____
_____
_____
_____
_____
_____
_____
_____
_____
_____
_____
_____
_____
_____
_____
_____
_____
_____

DAY 275

Ephesians 5:1-21

DAY 276

Ephesians 5:22-33

DAY 277

Ephesians 6

DAY 278

Philippians 1

DAY 279

Philippians 2

DAY 280

Philippians 3:1-4:1

DAY 281

Philippians 4:2-23

DAY 282

Colossians 1:1-23

DAY 283

Colossians 1:24-2:23

DAY 284

Colossians 3:1-4:1

DAY 285

Colossians 4:2-18

DAY 286

1 Thessalonians 1

DAY 287

1 Thessalonians 2:1-16

DAY 288

1 Thessalonians 2:17-3:13

DAY 289

1 Thessalonians 4

DAY 290

1 Thessalonians 5

DAY 291

2 Thessalonians 1

DAY 292

2 Thessalonians 2

DAY 293

2 Thessalonians 3

DAY 294

1 Timothy 1

DAY 295

1 Timothy 2

DAY 296

1 Timothy 3

DAY 297

1 Timothy 4

DAY 298

1 Timothy 5:1-6:2a

DAY 299

1 Timothy 6:2b-21

DAY 300

2 Timothy 1

DAY 301

2 Timothy 2

DAY 302

2 Timothy 3

DAY 303

2 Timothy 4

DAY 304

Titus 1

DAY 305

Titus 2

DAY 306

Titus 3

DAY 307

Philemon

DAY 308

Hebrews 1

DAY 309

Hebrews 2

DAY 310

Hebrews 3:1–4:13

DAY 311

Hebrews 4:14-5:10

DAY 312

Hebrews 5:11-612

DAY 313

Hebrews 6:13-7:10

DAY 314

Hebrews 7:11-28

DAY 315

Hebrews 8

DAY 316

Hebrews 9

DAY 317

Hebrews 10:1-18

DAY 318

Hebrews 10:19-39

DAY 319

Hebrews 11:1-16

DAY 320

Hebrews 11:17-40

DAY 321

Hebrews 12

DAY 322

Hebrews 13

DAY 323

James 1

DAY 324

James 2

DAY 325

James 3

DAY 326

James 4

DAY 327

James 5

DAY 328

1 Peter 1

DAY 329

1 Peter 2

DAY 330

1 Peter 3

DAY 331

1 Peter 4

DAY 332

1 Peter 5

DAY 333

2 Peter 1

DAY 334

2 Peter 2

DAY 335

2 Peter 3

DAY 336

1 John 1

DAY 337

1 John 2:1-27

DAY 338

1 John 2:28–3:24

_____
_____
_____
_____
_____
_____
_____
_____
_____
_____
_____
_____
_____
_____
_____
_____
_____
_____
_____
_____
_____
_____
_____
_____
_____

DAY 339

1 John 4

DAY 340

1 John 5

DAY 341

2 John

DAY 342

3 John

DAY 343

Jude

DAY 344

Revelation 1

DAY 345

Revelation 2

DAY 346

Revelation 3

DAY 347

Revelation 4

DAY 348

Revelation 5

_____
_____
_____
_____
_____
_____
_____
_____
_____
_____
_____
_____
_____
_____
_____
_____
_____
_____
_____
_____
_____
_____
_____
_____
_____

DAY 349

Revelation 6

_____
_____
_____
_____
_____
_____
_____
_____
_____
_____
_____
_____
_____
_____
_____
_____
_____
_____
_____
_____
_____
_____
_____
_____
_____

DAY 350

Revelation 7

_____

_____

_____

_____

_____

_____

_____

_____

_____

_____

_____

_____

_____

_____

_____

_____

_____

_____

_____

_____

_____

_____

_____

_____

_____

DAY 351

Revelation 8

DAY 352

Revelation 9

DAY 353

Revelation 10

DAY 354

Revelation 11

DAY 355

Revelation 12

DAY 356

Revelation 13

DAY 357

Revelation 14

DAY 358

Revelation 15

DAY 359

Revelation 16

DAY 360

Revelation 17

_____
_____
_____
_____
_____
_____
_____
_____
_____
_____
_____
_____
_____
_____
_____
_____
_____
_____
_____
_____
_____
_____
_____
_____
_____
_____
_____
_____

DAY 361

Revelation 18

DAY 362

Revelation 19

DAY 363

Revelation 20

DAY 364

Revelation 21

DAY 365

Revelation 22

Made in the USA
Las Vegas, NV
30 December 2023